THE BUSI

OWNER'S GUIDE TO

GOOGLE

SHOPPING

THE BUSINESS
OWNER'S GUIDE TO
GOOGLE
SHOPPING

How to do More with Less with
Google Shopping

MARK HAMMERSLEY

THE BUSINESS OWNER'S GUIDE TO GOOGLE SHOPPING
by MARK HAMMERSLEY

https://go.markhammersley.co/get-started

ISBN-13: 978-1-64370-880-5

TABLE OF CONTENTS

HOW TO DO MORE WITH LESS

Who Am I and Why Should You Care?

My name is Mark Hammersley, and I am not an aspiring author. While the world is full of people who long to become the spokespeople for a specific topic, I never thought about that. I just wanted to get things right for our clients. Okay, maybe I was looking for better results than that. I wanted to wow them. I wanted them to shake their heads in amazement when they experienced the results we brought to the table. Nothing can compete with results, so that's what I was after.

So, who am I again?

I run an ecommerce agency with offices based in Manchester and Auckland. We'd been growing our agency for about a decade when Google Shopping first sparked my interest. Back then it was called Froogle, and it was completely free. Some of our clients made their fortunes with it, and it fell within our SEO service at the time, so we were happy to work with it.

Since then, Google Shopping has been through much iteration, growing into the powerhouse it is today. When it was first introduced as a paid option, our agency threw some campaigns up there just to test the waters. We quickly noticed that Google Shopping worked extremely well for some of the clients who have previously failed with AdWords. These were primarily clients with higher priced products, and the success was due to the presentation. Instead of a flat description, searchers were now able to view a picture and price before they clicked through, thus filtering out the bargain hunters. We were satisfied with these newfound results for a short while, but we have a competitive nature, and we began running into people who were doing extremely well with Google Shopping: much better than we were! These individuals were getting 10 times the revenue normal campaigns would generate and spending less. We had to find out what they knew and become even better at it than they were. That was our goal.

This book is about our journey to discover the secrets that eventually allowed us to grow our campaigns by 10x and allow our clients to completely dominate Google Shopping, far surpassing their competition. (I told you we were competitive!)

There's a companion case study and video to this book that can be found here https://go.markhammersley.co/get-started. This will also allow me to update the video post publishing of this book as Google Shopping inevitably changes. Hence, if you want to know what's working right now, please get started by watching this video.

What Were We Trying to Do with Google Shopping?

Google Shopping is data driven. This lent itself well to our expertise, having fifteen developers and an expert-level technical AdWords team. Based on prior experience, we already knew that every new marketing channel has hidden loopholes that have the potential to make the people who discover them lots of money. For example, someone discovers a special technique with Amazon Marketplace selling, and during the five years it takes for the market to catch up, this person is enjoying huge market share growth. I believe we are still within the golden age of Google Shopping, meaning that most of the market is still completely in the dark, and a few smart retailers are reaping tremendous benefits.

Yes, totally in the dark.

You wouldn't believe how many accounts I see that consist of one campaign, one ad group, and one bid. Often, because Google works, these campaigns make money, but they could be doing so much better.

Those Annoying 'Google Shopping Experts'

To be honest, whenever I met someone at a digital marketing event who was doing amazing in Google Shopping it really annoyed me. Here was someone who'd been working on ecommerce for less time than me, with less AdWords experience than I had, but doing better. My ego just couldn't handle it, so I became obsessed. I befriended these people, paid for them to coach me, bought them lunch, got them drunk, anything to help me find out how to crack their secrets. Each person gave me a little more information until my shopping campaigns took off like a rocket; but hats off to all these pioneers. I just hope they will forgive me when I share their secrets!

The War

But it was not all smooth sailing. It wasn't a case of just cloning everyone I met. A lot of people who thought they cracked it had only done so for their own product set, or just got lucky, and thought they knew something they really didn't. When we tested their methods across our campaigns, things often got worse! In fact, after experimenting for six months, I began to believe it was hopeless to try and beat the system, that Google's machine learning was just better than me and to leave it there.

The Epiphany

But then a few things happened. One, I watched the 2014 presentation on Google Shopping Tiers, which opened my mind to the belief that people could scale much higher with Google Shopping. Then, I listened to the CEO of Whoop talk. Both these approaches gave me the boost I needed to start my mental wheels turning again. Some of my structure I owe to these guys for sharing, and I thank them for providing a good foundation to work from. What I liked were the revenue increase charts and the reasons behind their growth. What was also very clear from their presentations was that these guys were only just scratching the surface with what they were doing. So, either they were holding a lot back or they hadn't quite taken the next step of connecting the dots.

Regardless of which it was, I knew I had to get to work.

The Plan

Luckily, I have plenty of clients over a wide range of industries to test with. I also have complete control over the shopping feed. Our whole operation became a giant laboratory. The best way to move forward was to use some of the accounts as the control group to test the different structures and techniques, keeping what worked and discarding what didn't.

The Pain

However, these are real live ecommerce accounts, and I have monthly goals to reach for each one. I couldn't afford poor results with everyone depending on me to grow the revenue of our client's sites. When I rolled out one expert technique that involved a single product Ad group with one product ID per Ad group, I thought I was on to something.

Not so. All my accounts promptly died.

Not wanting to panic, I reasoned that Google must be getting used to the new structure, so I waited. Clients were freaking out, and after a month of decreasing impression share, I rolled back. I thought that messing around would just make things worse, but I happened to notice that one account improved on that structure. So, my focus became on why that account worked on this structure and why the others burned. It was this difference that gave me the first clue to cracking the secret.

The Achievement

With the techniques I'm about to share with you, we have experienced phenomenal results with Google Shopping! To give you a taste of the results you can hope to achieve by implementing some of this stuff, I am going to share one of our case studies for the work we did with a company selling castors.

30.87% REVENUE INCREASE YEAR ON YEAR FROM A 40.68% REDUCTION IN SPEND

This site sells a large range of castors and wheels, primarily B2B but also some B2C. When I took over the account, the spend was high, but the return on spend was low. My focus, of course, was on reducing spend while increasing revenue. There was a lot of wasted spend to go after and perfect for my techniques.

Here is a selection of their products on Google Shopping:

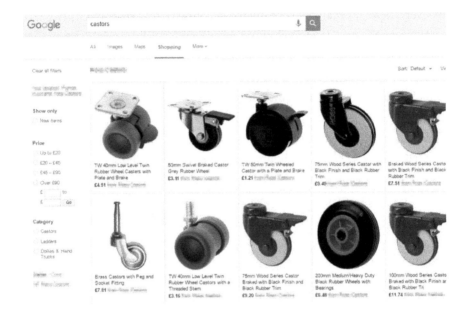

The results after implementation:

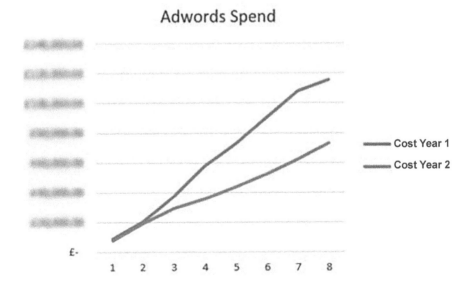

Massive reduction in Google Shopping spend:

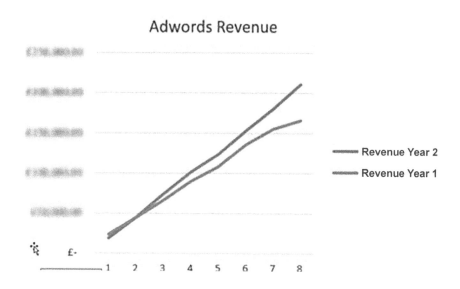

Large reduction in spend while increasing Google Shopping search revenue, other stats:

Clicks	Cost	CPC	Sessions	Bounce Rate
27.18% ⬆	40.68% ⬇	53.36% ⬆	26.39% ⬆	0.61% ⬇

Bounce rate and transactions:

Bounce Rate	Pages/Session	E-commerce Conversion Rate	Transactions	Revenue
0.61% ⬇	3.51% ⬇	2.79% ⬆	29.91% ⬆	30.87% ⬆

Next, take a look at how these techniques worked with a website that sells cookware.

Revenue year on year over Christmas:

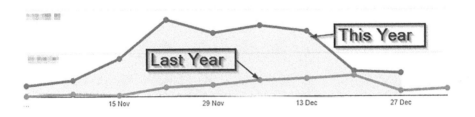

Benefit:

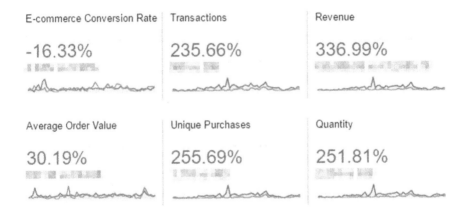

A slight conversion rate drop but worth it due to the higher increase in average order value.

And again, for another client selling baby products:

Revenue & Conversion Rate		Transactions	
Revenue	E-commerce Conversion Rate	Transactions	Average Order Value
Google Shopping Adword...	Google Shopping Adword...	Google Shopping Adword...	Google Shopping Adword...
65.13%	3.07%	35.78%	21.61%

It's so good when you find something that works!

These methods work for clothing websites too, see below:

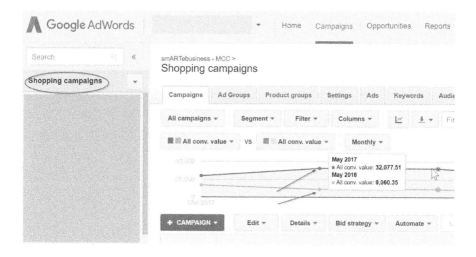

And also home decor:

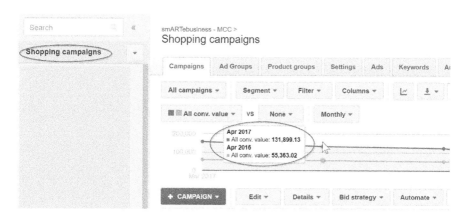

And across many industries, including B2B websites.

SO WHAT IS GOOGLE SHOPPING

Just in case you don't know what Google Shopping is, I want to explain what this marketing channel is. We are primarily talking about the Google Search ads that look like these

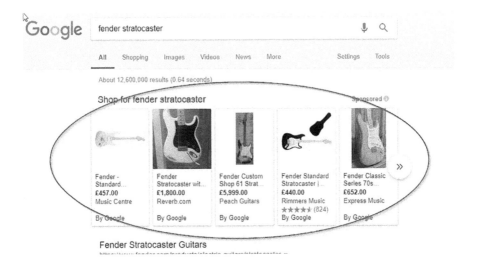

Fender Stratocaster Guitars

If you search for a product on Google, then typically you see results like the above. The search result shows you the product image, the product title, the price and the company selling the product. Also the product might have some review stars on it or a special offer.

What's more, if you click on the Shopping Tab, you get to see a wider selection of these products

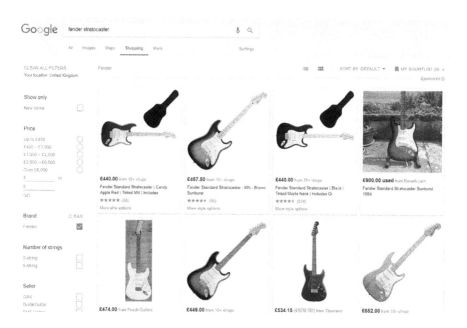

This channel is becoming really big business for Google and also for ecommerce sites, so you really want to know how to get the top results from this.

It all starts with a retailer who wants to get their products into Google. They have a lot of information about those products such as product titles, pricing, descriptions, images, etc. Based on that, a retailer will put together a product feed of all the product data which looks something like this

This is basically a list of all the products on a website, the links of the products, their image link, descriptions and all the information Google will need to promote that product.

This product feed which is usually in a comma separated or XML file format then goes into the Google Merchant Centre.

The Google Merchant Centre really allows us to check the products, make sure there are no errors and that Google is happy with the structure of it. This is Google's quality control centre to make sure that everything that should be in order is in order.

Once you have got that set up, then you can use the Google Merchant Centre to get those products into Google AdWords.

So that's essentially a data dump into Google AdWords, and of course, next we need to start structuring those products in a meaningful way in AdWords. This is because we want to be bidding and spending money on different areas of the product selection.

Let me give you an example of someone selling sport training shoes. So, they might start by splitting things down by brand:

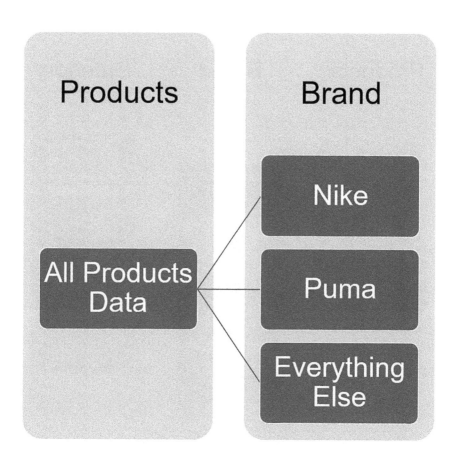

And then by category:

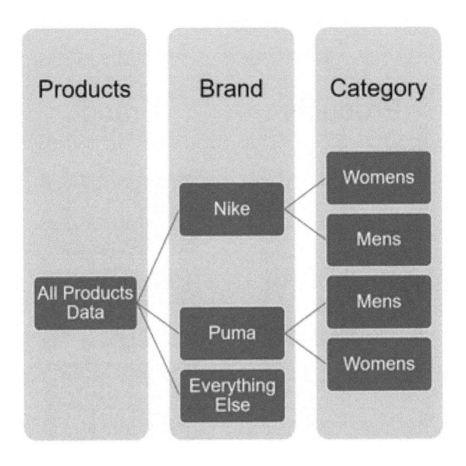

These different levels are called product groups.

Then at the final level, you would probably split the categories by product ID:

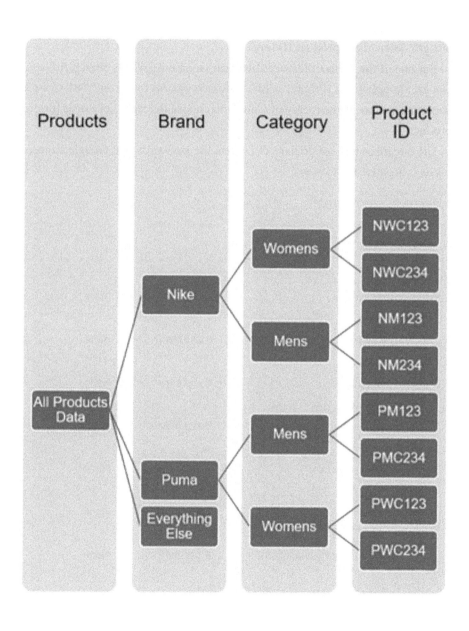

This gives you a lot of freedom on how you want to structure the account and ultimately where you want to spend your money.

We do this structure so that we can bid differently on different products: i.e., you might want to set your bid at the 'Nike' level, the 'Womens' category level or right down at the product ID level.

But one of the main differences between Google AdWords Search Ads and Google Shopping Ads is that we don't choose keywords to bid on. With Google Shopping, we are at the mercy of Google to choose the right keywords for our products.

The one main tool we do have to control the keywords that Google chooses for us is negative keywords:

Search term	↑	Match Type ?	Added / Excluded ?
Total			
10 ml syringe		Exact match	None
100 ml beaker		Exact match	None
10ml syringes		Exact match	None
4 20ma output		Exact match	None
4 20ma ph sensor		Exact match	None
5ml syringe		Exact match	None
6.86 ph calibration solution		Exact match	None
60 ml syringes for sale		Exact match	None
60ml syringe		Exact match	None

So, if we looked at the keywords above, we might negative out the keyword (search term) '5ml syringe' because we know that we don't sell 5ml syringes or perhaps we are getting a lot of traffic from this term, and it's too generic, and it's never converting into a sale:

Search term	↑	Match Type ?	Added / Excluded ?
Total			
10 ml syringe		Exact match	None
100 ml beaker		Exact match	None
10ml syringes		Exact match	None
4 20ma output		Exact match	None
4 20ma ph sensor		Exact match	None
5ml syringe		Exact match	None
6.86 ph calibration solution		Exact match	None
60 ml syringes for sale		Exact match	None
60ml syringe		Exact match	None

We can use negative keywords to give us a little bit more control on what we are bidding on.

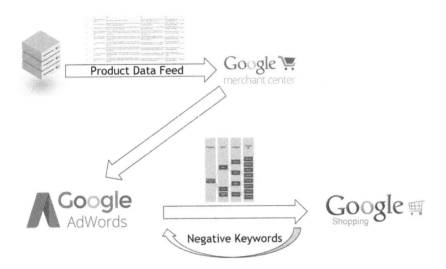

On the most basic level, this is how most Google Shopping setups are run and managed.

There are three areas where we can optimise Google Shopping, and these are as follows:

- **Product Feed Optimisation** – making the feed perform better by changing elements to increase conversions, click through rate and impression share.
- **Bid Management** – changing bids based on past sales history of a product group or product ID, predicting bids based on upcoming promotions, essentially trying to bid to get more sales for less spend.
- **Campaign Tiers** – using campaign levels to sculpt the search queries so that certain queries get bid higher and some bid lower depending on past results.

This book is about how to optimise these three areas to take your Google Shopping results to the next level.

HOW TO USE THIS BOOK

I realize that the people reading this book are going to be at various levels in their knowledge and growth with Google Shopping campaigns. Because of this, I want to provide an overview of what I am going to cover, so you can quickly understand where you are going to get the most value.

Firstly, I cover **Campaign Structure** and how to structure the basics, looking at how you might build out certain product groups and why. We also look at when you should branch off a campaign into its own campaign, gaining more control over budget and targeting for a set of products.

We then go a little deeper to look at **Tiered Campaigns**, how they work and why you might want to use them. This is the start of a solid technique that allows you to control your keyword bidding. We also look at single product ad groups to determine if this might help you with your setup.

After building the foundation, we dive into the **Penthouse Strategy**, which is what has allowed me to grow a lot of my accounts.

Once we have the structure nailed and keywords are being bid on well, products that excel are given rocket fuel. Next, we turn our attention to **Feed Optimisation Techniques**, where we look at product titles, product descriptions and product images. This should allow you to grab more impression share, leading us next to the use of **Custom Labels** to help understand whether you want those extra impressions and, if so, on which products: basically, giving you the most important information where the action is, in AdWords, rather than in the ecommerce store back end.

By this stage, you might be thinking 'How Can I Manage all this?!' so I want to cover some **Third-Party Tools** to use to increase insight and efficiency.

We also need to go through the bidding strategy and the idiosyncrasies of this as it will greatly affect your return on Ad spend.

We will cover a lot more, but the above is the main thrust of the book.

Are you ready?

INSIDE A CAMPAIGN

One of the most important tasks to work out is how to split up your product groups. This is accomplished by using what's available in your shopping feed. For example, you're only going to be able to split the product groups by category if the category is represented in the product feed. Often, the product feed doesn't contain all the information you would like to have to split the account down. Therefore, you might need to do some work on this.

To work out the best way to split the product groups, you'll have to think ahead about how the account is going to grow over time. If you want to branch out a high performing set of products into a new campaign to give them their own budget, then the initial structure is going to either help or hinder this goal. If you don't have product groups split down in the way you might later want to split shopping campaigns, then you might need to redo your base campaigns to accommodate this change. This can become a bit tedious, as your base campaign will have bid history and different bidding per products, etc., along with product groups, which you would need to recreate. It's best to have a good idea of how you might want to split it before you start. Don't worry. You'll start thinking with the end in sight once you have a clear picture of how it all works together.

With that said, there is one basic rule I always use for the last product group and that's to let the most granular level be the product ID itself. Having the product groups split on the last step by the product ID means that you can have individual bids for each individual product. This is important as Pareto's rule usually applies, and 20% of the products generate 80% of the profits. Having individual bids means that you can bid up products doing well and bid down products performing poorly.

Here are the fields in a datafeed that you can use to split a campaign:

- Brand of Items
- Category of Items
- Google Category
- Price Level (higher than £50, lower than)
- Bestseller Status
- Margin of Item
- Price Competitiveness
- Lifetime Value of an Item

When starting an account, I tend to only use the first three. If there's a wide variety of Google Categories, then I might split differently. For example, one of our clients is an ecommerce store with a variety of baby products. cross over quite a few different categories. It makes sense to align with Goog and give them the products in groups that Google understands. Then I would further split the products by brand and not use the category as this should mirror the Google Category.

Some sites don't have a lot of Google Categories available to them, so splitting at this level doesn't make sense. For example, a car parts site would likely have products that end up falling into only one or two Google Categories.

Other ecommerce sites carry a lot of different brands, and if this is the case, splitting off by brand on the first tier is sensible as it's likely that the retailer is able to sell certain brands better than others. For example, perhaps they can buy these products cheaper than others or they have a wider range in stock or they can deliver them faster or have a better reputation for customer support on these products. If there is an advantage to selling a particular brand and it's getting decent impressions, then it would make sense to move these brands into their own campaign. So, splitting at brand level in the base campaign makes sense. I would then further refine the product groups by category of item so that if a brand spans across multiple categories we can split out this subsection later as well. For example, a brand might do well in one category but not another, so you wouldn't want to spend more budget on the brand in the low performing category areas.

Once you split off the products that are doing well into other campaigns, then you can dig deeper into the impression share that you're getting and try to improve this. If you're making good ROAS (return on advertising spend) on certain products, then you want to increase the impression share of that product to the maximum.

Other retailers only sell their own brand. In this case, I would split by category and then product ID. This should show you the products that are performing well and can be split off when needed.

Further refinement of the account can come later when you have more data. Then you can start to play with some of the categories I previously mentioned:

- Price Level (higher than 50, lower than)
- Bestseller Status
- Margin of Item
- Price Competitiveness
- Lifetime Value of an Item

favourites is the lifetime value of an item. For example, itamin supplements – some products will have monthly ve the data on lifetime value against SKU then you can ing feed (for Magento our Scent Trail tracking product would want to sell more of the products that have high lifetime values, so you'd set rules to split the lifetime value figure into bracket such as:

- LTCV is less than $25
- LTCV is less than $50
- LTCV is less than $75
- LTCV is less than $100
- LTCV is greater than $100

If you have this data, I would split this in the following way:

Brand Product Group > Category Product Group > LTCV Tier Product Group > Product ID

This way, when you are setting your bids on the products, you can easily see if the product is a high repeat business product. If it is, you might accept a lower ROAS to get the sale.

See how that works?

Using lifetime value for customers that are guaranteed repeat buys is key. Retailers like the following would benefit massively:

- Contact lens retailers
- Clothing retailers
- Fishing retailers (and other sporting goods, like golf)
- Protein and bodybuilding type shops
- Online food retailers

There are countless more – basically any business where the repeat purchase rate per customer is on average greater than 1.5.

If the retailer has massively differing margins on different products, then this is a useful custom label to add to the product feed. Again, in the following format:

Brand Product Group > Category Product Group > Profit Margin Tier Product Group > Product ID

This way you'll have the information on the customer margin right at the point where you're choosing the correct bid.

One point to make here though is the way Google Shopping works with product groups. As the data in the feed for values (such as lifetime value) will be updated and changing, often the product groups that a product is in might change from week to week. Unfortunately, if the value of the custom value changes (and this means that the product should move to a new product group) Google will not make this change automatically. In such a case, you'll either have to move the products manually to the new group (not practical), do this via scripting in the bulk operations area or you'll have to use a third-party tool like Optmyzr.

Confused?

Okay, I've just covered a lot of different ways to structure a campaign, but it doesn't need to be so complicated, especially if you're just getting started. Let me take you through the steps I took to structure a recent menswear client.

This client sells men's clothing split down into various categories. The categories split down into sub groups, but the main categories are Suits, Jackets. Shirts and Trousers. I used these as my main starting product groups.

- Product Group 1 – Suits
- Product Group 2 – Jackets
- Product Group 3 – Shirts
- Product Group 4 – Everything else

I then split each product group into further refined product groups, and was done simply into Product IDs. If they had sold different brands, I would have split further into brands before splitting into product groups.

That's it to start with. Always start simple and build up later based on results. You can add your bestseller campaign later, get into tiers, but first, you want to make sure you can make some sales. If there's not a sniff of sales, then all the crazy optimisation is not going to help. Make sure your shop has a good product market fit, look at pricing, offer incentive, positioning and all the ecommerce conversion rate stuff that we cover in our other book.

When to Split Off Some Products into a New Campaign

If you have a very successful range of products selling well in the main shopping campaign and getting at least 50 sales in 30 days, that's the time to split this off into its own campaign.

The benefit of doing this:

- These products might sell better at different times of the week compared to the bulk of other products, so you might want to use bid modifiers for the best times of day and week.
- These products might sell better in certain locations than the rest of the products, so you might want to bid differently in different locations.
- You might want to assign more budget to these products.
- If the monthly budget is running tight, you might want to just run these higher performing ROAS products and drop the main shopping search campaign.

So how do you know when to split off some products into their own campaign?

Here are some rules of thumb:

- If a product group is generating more than 30% of the revenue, then I would consider splitting this out.
- But only if that product group is experiencing at least 50 conversions a month. Any lower and it won't benefit from the Google Shopping Algorithm later.

The above is all basic, and I go into a lot more detail in the section called Increasing Impression Share, which is where we get into the really cool stuff.

STRUCTURING CAMPAIGNS FOR MAXIMUM EFFECT

Now, I want to cover how to use campaign structure together to take advantage of different search terms for different keywords and how to harness the best Google AI tools for the right products. But before I do this, I need to introduce tiered campaigns and SPAG – single product ad groups.

Are you ready?

Tiered Campaigns for Keyword Bidding

In 2014, there was an interesting presentation on using tiered campaigns entitled 'Taking Google Shopping to the Next Level' by Martin Roettgerding. The video can be seen here:

https://goo.gl/z4hEip

This is an exciting way to use the 'priority' settings of the Google Shopping campaigns to bid differently on different keywords. I use this method as a good starting point on all my shopping campaigns combined with Google AdWords scripting to automate the process of moving up and down keywords.

The normal structure for a shopping campaign forces you to select a bid for a product that will apply for all keywords.

Let's use an example to explain this:

In a campaign, we are selling tennis racquets, and we have our product groups refined down to product ID. Tennis racquet 'Prince TeXtreme Premier 120' could trigger an impression for the following search queries:

- 'tennis racquets'
- 'prince tennis racquets'
- 'prince TeXtreme tennis racquet'

As you can see, we are much more likely to convert on the last keyword as it is very specific to the brand of tennis racquet we are selling. The searcher is likely to be ready to purchase. However, a high bid would encourage a lot of impressions on the generic 'tennis racquets' search query. Our only option would be to negative out the generic 'tennis racquets' so that we don't spend on generic terms.

This is not optimal because we might want generic tennis racquet keywords if we could get the clicks at a very low cost. Also, we would want to bid more on 'Prince TeXtreme tennis racquet' than we bid on 'Prince tennis racquets.'

In order to bid differently on different search terms for the same product IDs, we need to move to a tiered campaign structure for shopping search campaigns. This is done using the Shopping Campaign priority setting.

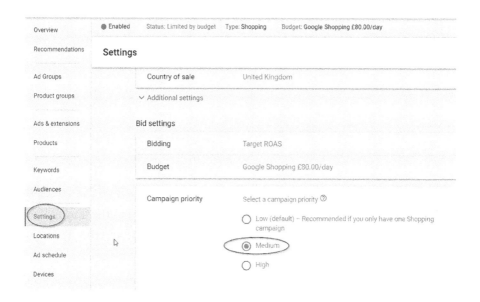

Without this setting, if we had multiple campaigns with the same 'campaign priority' and the same products, then Google would use the campaign with the products with the highest bid to show the impression. But we want a lower bid on certain keywords and higher bids on others.

I tend to set this up in the following way:

- Catch All Campaign – priority medium
- Low Bid Campaign – priority low
- High Bid Campaign – priority low

I use one campaign to hunt for keywords, and then based on the stats, I'll either leave them in the 'catch all' campaign or move them to the 'low bid' or 'high bid' campaigns. The catch all is set as priority 'medium,' and the other two have priority 'low'. All these campaigns have exactly the same product group split, but they have different bids on those product groups.

Once the above it set up, I use 'shared negative' lists to move keywords up and down depending on conversion value over cost results. For example, if I was spending a lot on 'tennis racquets' then I would move this down into the low-bid campaign. If I was getting a good amount of sales on 'Xtreme Prince Racquet' and I wanted a higher impression share, I would move this to the high bid campaign.

This gives you much more flexibility on product bids and helps you focus on the top terms while still utilising the cheaper more generic terms that may convert.

With this setup, you also want to use a shared budget across your Low, Medium and High Campaigns – otherwise you could have the Low and Medium run out of daily budget, meaning that the High Campaign got all the traffic and bid high on everything! Not good.

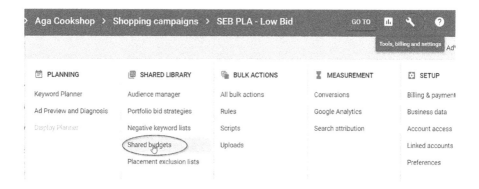

When starting out and the structure is still quite simple, you can utilize saved filters with set parameters on the search queries to designate which keywords should be moved up and down.

These filters can have thresholds, such as number of clicks and conversion value over cost.

The above is the filter I used to see which search terms are doing well and need to graduate from my Low Bid campaign.

Once you have a solid understanding of what you're doing and are confident about managing this process, i.e., how often you move keywords up and down and how you bid product bids up and down, this whole process can be scripted. Scripting allows you to easily create much more granular campaigns than you could create manually. With scripting, you can have tiers running for each device category while product categories are running in their own campaigns for better budget allocation. Doing it all manually can get confusing fast!

Medium Tail and Short Tail

Within each tiered campaign, I split the ad groups into two. One is called Medium Tail and the other Short Tail. The Medium Tail ad group is the ad group that gets most of the traffic as it has a higher bid than the Short Tail ad group. I usually start with the Short Tail ad group set at a bid of 25% less than the medium tail.

Splitting out the ad groups like this allows me to negative out the longer tail keywords into the Short Tail campaign or to push lower click through rate keywords into the Short Tail campaign. This, along with the tiered campaigns, allows me to effectively have six levels of slots for a keyword and thus have six levels of bid for each product for different keywords.

Here's the example:

Low Bid:
- Short Tail – e.g., search term 'prams'
- Medium Tail – e.g., search term 'twin prams'

Medium Bid (catch all):
- Short Tail – e.g., search term 'mima'
- Medium Tail – e.g., search term 'mima pram'

High Bid:
- Short Tail – e.g., search term 'twin mima pram 2017'
- Medium Tail – e.g., search term 'blue mima twin pram 2017'

At first, you won't need all these levels, and you should only add these levels if you see search terms for products that you would like to split up like this. But as you grow you can build up to this until there is no need to go further. Some markets don't have that much granularity, and you can just use the Penthouse Strategy (explained below) without the Medium Tail and Short Tail slots.

A good way to find keywords that you would use in the Short Tail ad group is to look at click through rate and search queries that have had more than a certain amount of impressions. For example, I have this filter setup to search for short tail keywords:

Here we are looking for search terms that are getting lower than 1% click through rate, impressions of over 200 and a conversion value / cost of less than 4. I use this with a 30-day time frame. If this shows up, I can negative out some of the search terms at ad group level, forcing them to show in the lower bid Short Tail ad group.

Because I am using CTR as the guiding factor here, I can move search terms more quickly than waiting on their overall 'conversion value / cost' figure: i.e., they move more quickly to a lower bid campaign to ensure my ad groups CTR rate is kept high. This also allows me to see the forest for the trees and decide if I want these short tail search terms at any cost. It's quicker than waiting to move it down to the low bid campaign, so it limits the damage poor search terms can do to the main revenue generators.

One Ad Group per Product ID

When I first heard the idea of having one ad group per product ID, I thought it was brilliant! I saw it like this; because of the negative keywords you can have at ad group level, you could control which search term came up for which products. That's perfect because if a search term doesn't work for one product it might work for another one. I was able to build out the campaign and ad groups easily using Optmyzr; however, maintaining these ad groups was impossible manually. Just think about it: new products get added all the time, and you must constantly create new ad groups for these products.

But there's always a solution, right?

We solved this through scripting. The script ran each day and looked for new products, adding them into new ad groups. It was all looking good; however, on all but one of the accounts I used this idea on, my impression share took a massive dive. Google can take up to three weeks to get used to a new structure, so I waited, but the impressions never returned. Given this, I had no choice but to abandon this technique. However, other people seem to have success with this structure.

What was I doing wrong?

The reason my campaigns died is because the CTR of the ad groups is important to the overall impression share of the ad group, which I will go into later when talking about impression share. Therefore, just opting for single product ad groups (SPAGs) for all campaigns you manage is a lottery – you really need to see how the CTR flows across all products. If you find that CTR is similar and the top revenue products all have decent CTR, then SPAGs can potentially work well. But I don't use them anymore.

The Penthouse Strategy

Over everything else written in this book, this structure has been the most beneficial, allowing me to really grow my accounts. It combines a structure, which once set up tailors itself to the strengths of Google and allows you to push winners hard and increase ROAS on low cost generic search terms.

A word of warning though: the Penthouse Strategy will only work if you have some truly highly converting, highly optimized products. You might be lucky to have products that can be pushed into the Penthouse straight away and have everything run smoothly, but if you try the Penthouse Strategy and it doesn't increase your conversion, this is a sign that your products need more optimisation. Think of this as a PLAN, DO, CHECK, ACT cycle:

- **Plan** – Get ready to try the Penthouse Strategy by identifying the eligible products.
- **Do** – Try the Penthouse Strategy with the qualifying products.
- **Check** – Did it work? Did the account increase in revenue while maintaining Conversion Value over Cost; or did it fail?
- **Act** – If the experiment failed, go back and work on optimising your top products. For example: make sure they have plenty of reviews and stars on the Google Shopping image. Do price matching on competitors. Optimize the titles, images, and promotions. Repeat the cycle.

The Penthouse Strategy will only work well if you have a few Olympian products that can carry their weight in the Penthouse. So, if this doesn't work on the first try, focus your efforts on making your top five products more optimized, then retry. This means your efforts are working on products that already have a shot at being excellent producers.

The Penthouse Strategy works like this – first, you have your tiered campaign structure as described before, but these all sit at priority levels:

- low bid – low priority
- high bid – low priority

- catch all – medium priority

This leaves the High Priority slot empty and allows you to put a bestseller campaign on top of the tiered campaign.

Settings

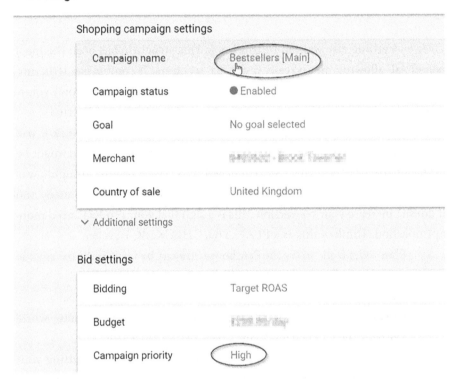

Shopping campaign settings

Campaign name	Bestsellers [Main]
Campaign status	● Enabled
Goal	No goal selected
Merchant	
Country of sale	United Kingdom

∨ Additional settings

Bid settings

Bidding	Target ROAS
Budget	
Campaign priority	High

So, think of a hotel: you have all your low-paying guests in your not so fancy rooms (low bid), no sea views, etc. Then you have your highest paying guests in your sea view rooms and your normal guests in your medium catch all quality rooms. But what about those VIP high paying guests who are willing to pay so much more than your normal customer? You'd put them in the special penthouse suite, right? They tend to get about four times the space of a normal room as they are worth so much more.

		Campaign	Budget	Status
☐	◉			

Total: All but removed campaigns ⑦

			Campaign	Budget	Status
☐	●	◪	Shopping Level 2 [Main]		Eligible
☐	●	◪	Shopping Level 3 [Main]		Eligible
☐	●	◪	Shopping Low Bid [Main]		Eligible
☐	●	◪	Bestsellers [Main]		Eligible

By putting a bestseller campaign on top of your tiered campaigns, you get to promote your best products and take off all the constraints and allow them to fly high.

To find which products I want to put into the bestseller campaign, I set a criterion of sales in the tiered campaigns and then move up and down to the bestseller campaign based on this. For example, any products that have sold more than three times during the past 30 days can be promoted to the Penthouse to see how they perform. If they don't do well, they get moved back down to the lower tiers.

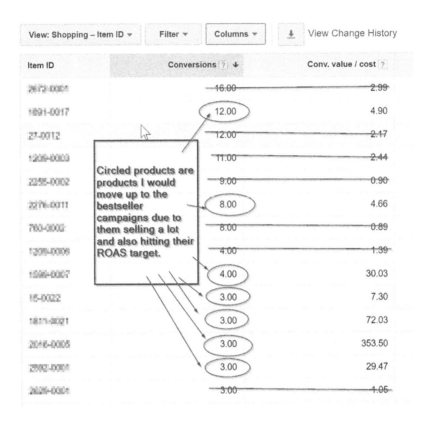

Because this Penthouse campaign is the best of the best, Google's bid strategies work much better with them. For the tiered campaigns, I tend to use manual CPC without the enhanced box checked, so I have more control (although this is changing for me in 2018 as the AI gets better). But for the Penthouse, Google's machine learning algorithms work so much better for higher performing products. It's understandable since Google's bid strategies are built by Google, so they're bound to be tipped in their favour. Their goal is to support Google's overall objective, which is to raise ad spend, thus it's best to let them do this only with your best products and only when they are selling well.

Here is a recent example of the implementation of the Penthouse Strategy, the only reason it dipped at the end is because of month end and budget constraints! But, as you can see, the revenue was so much higher for only a small increase in spend. Exciting stuff, right? And I I've seen this repeated across numerous accounts.

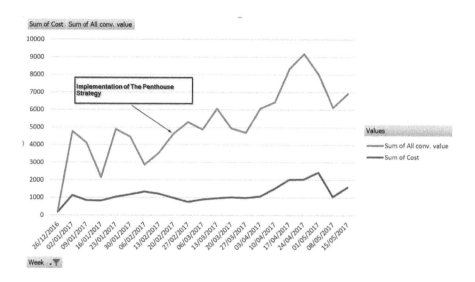

To refine further, you can also split your bestseller campaign into the normal Short Tail and Medium Tail ad groups. This way you can avoid bidding too high on some of the generic terms in your market.

Once you have this structure nailed down, you can start using AdWords Scripting to automate most of it; however, at first, this is easy to do manually. Just check the products that are selling well each week and make any necessary changes. Once this is scripted, you can spend your time optimising the product feed. If you think about it, product feed optimisation is the one thing that Google cannot control. They can't select different images for the product. They can't change product titles. So, as Google gets better at their side of the Google Shopping, we as AdWords managers, are going to have to move more and more into feed optimisation to help Google do its job by providing better data.

FEED OPTIMISATION
TECHNIQUES

Next, we are going to dig into Feed Optimisation techniques. This and the products that are in the feed are going to become the battleground of the future. As Google's artificial intelligence becomes better and better, our job as marketers is going to be making sure that what's going into Google is the best it can be. First, we will look at **Product Titles** as these in my experiments have been one of the best places to effect impression share and ultimately conversions. This leads on nicely to **Product Descriptions**, which has less of an effect but is important in markets where Google is really struggling to match the search query to the right product (for example, 'car parts').

Then we will be talking about how to optimize products for different search queries, which can be important if one or two products drive the lion's share on the Google Shopping Revenue. How people use search intent also will affect your results, and I cover my theories on this.

Of course, the big one, **Product Images** make or break the sale. Each product image tells a thousand words, but what those words are will dictate your success, so I show you how you can semi-split test these.

We are also diving into **Pricing, Use of Offers, Promotions** and **Custom Labels to Give You an Edge** and showing you how to test all these. Feel free to jump ahead to the section that you are most interested in!

Product Titles

Often in your Google Shopping feed, the product titles are just taken straight from the product titles on the website. The potential problem here is that sometimes what's good for the website is not so great for Google Shopping. In terms of relevance to a search query, the product title ranks up there highly as a signal whether a product is relevant or not. Google takes the product title from left to right in order of importance, so the keyword that you want to rank for should be placed as close to the left as possible.

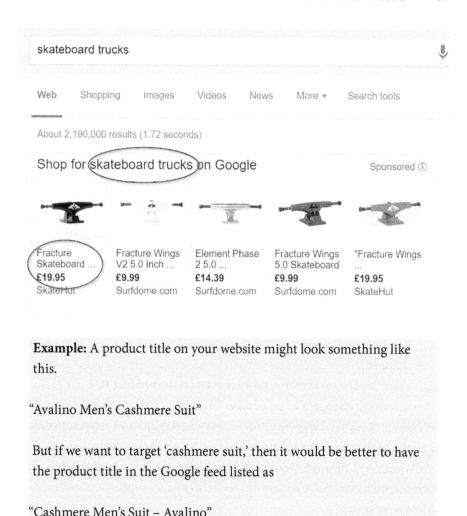

Example: A product title on your website might look something like this.

"Avalino Men's Cashmere Suit"

But if we want to target 'cashmere suit,' then it would be better to have the product title in the Google feed listed as

"Cashmere Men's Suit – Avalino"

See how that works?

Sometimes this creates a conflict between what the site needs and what's optimal for Google. We've worked around this by changing the product title in the Google Product Feed and then dynamically changing the website product title to match the feed when a visitor comes to the site. By doing this, all normal website traffic sees the default product title, but the Google Shopping traffic sees whatever we have in the feed. This means we can use our testing tools to uncover the best product title without having to change the product title in the website's admin area.

The best way to know what set of words to use as your product title will be from using that data in your search query reports. This is particularly effective if you use the 'one product id' per ad group structure that we talk about later in this book – as with this structure you can see which keywords each product is appearing for and how it's converting. Thus, if you see that a product is converting well for a certain keyword, you can optimize the product title further to try to gain more impressions for that product.

Unfortunately, within the Google AdWords interface it's quite hard to work out the impact of the change to a product title. Here is the manual process:

1. Make the change to the product title.
2. Wait about 15 days to let some stats build up.
3. Go into the dimensions report and pull off the impressions, clicks, sales, etc., against Product ID – do this for the 15 days before the change and then again for the 15 days after the change and pull both these data sets into Excel.
4. Look up the product ID in the feed to find the product that you've changed.
5. Compare the two before and after stats on the product IDs.

If you want to change a large number of product titles and you're doing it often, this process can be quite burdensome and difficult to keep track of. But this is one of the best ways to optimize sales. To get around this, I applied for an AdWords API through Google and built a tool that tracks the before and after changes.

More solutions!

It looks like this:

Id	Title	Days Since Change	Impressions		CTR		Clicks		CPC		Converions		Conversion Value	
			Before	After	Before	After	Before	After	Before	After	Before	After	Before	After
397	Adjustable Feet - M8 x 50 Rigid with 38mm base M8 x 50 Rigid Adjustable foot with a 38mm base	8	979.62	826.12	2.07	2.09	19.15	16.88	0.60	0.50	1.28	1.25	23.07	16.22
914	4 Rubber Wheels / Castors - 100mm Swivel & Grey Rubber 4 Rubber Castors - 100mm Swivel Castrot Grey Rubber Castor Wheel	6	386.76	160.00	1.98	1.07	6.34	2.17	0.31	0.43	0.26	0.33	7.77	4.81

So, if you're going to be doing a lot of product title changes, then building a tool like this is going to help significantly. You can see the before product title on the left, in smaller font, underneath the after product title.

(In the above example, both changes seem worse!)

If you are only managing one account, you can monitor changes in the feed manually. It's only if you are a testing freak like me that you need to build yourself a tool!

Product Titles when Selling Known Brands

If your store sells branded products, like Le Creuset frying pans, make sure the brand name is the first part of your product title. Often this is the case by default, but some stores don't do this and could be losing impressions due to the missing brand identifier in the product title even though it may already be in the Brand field in the feed.

How do you structure product titles? I suggest that product titles are optimized differently for different industries.

Clothing:
- Brand: Gender: Product Name: Color: Size: Material
- Brook Taverner Men's Epsom Suit – Blue 48" Wool

Consumer Goods:
- Brand: Product Name: Weight, Count etc.
- Maxi Pea Protein – 5 kg, 20 servings

Furniture:
- Brand: Product Name: Features (Size, Material, Quantity)
- Trade Tested Generators – 200 KW, Low Noise, Economy

Electronics:
- Brand: Attributes: Product Name: Model Number
- Sony 50" LED Bravia TV with 4k flat screen (UN5326435T)

Seasonal:
- Occasion: Product Name: Attributes
- Valentine's Day Personalised LoveHearts Sweets

Books:
- Title: Type: Format (hardcover eBook) + Author
- Jamie's 15 Minute Meals Delicious, Nutritious, Super-Fast Food Hardcover – Jamie Oliver

However, there are no hard and fast rules for this, and even though a lot of these title format recommendations come from Google themselves, it makes sense to change it around. For example, not all brands are well known enough to boost click through, and thus a benefit/feature might be better coming first.

How To Find What Search Queries Are Pulling Up Which Product IDs

If you want more impressions, optimising the product title to include more of the relevant search queries will help. Not only will Google give you more of the impression share but the click through rate should be higher due to the 'keyword' 'product title' match.

You can find out what product IDs are coming up for what search queries; however, it is a little hidden away. Of course, I have figured out a process to show you how to pull off this information!

By now you should know how my brain works, right? (However, please note this little hack only seems to work in the old AdWords interface, and at the time of writing, that's still available.)

This trick will only work, however, if your product groups are refined down to product ID level. If they are only refined down to brand or category, then you will only see search queries against these.

Here are the steps:

First, select the date range you want to pull this information off for and then select the Dimensions tab at the All Campaigns level of the account.

In the View drop down, select Search Terms.

Next, you'll want to filter the Search Terms to include only those of the Google Shopping campaigns. To do this, usually your shopping campaigns have something in their name that is different than the search campaign, so you can do it that way.

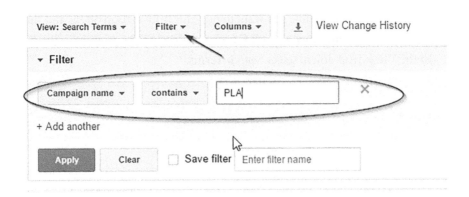

In the case above, all this client's Google Shopping Campaigns have the letters *PLA* in them, and therefore, we can hone in on them this way.

Next, you want to click on the Columns button and bring in the Keywords column, like below.

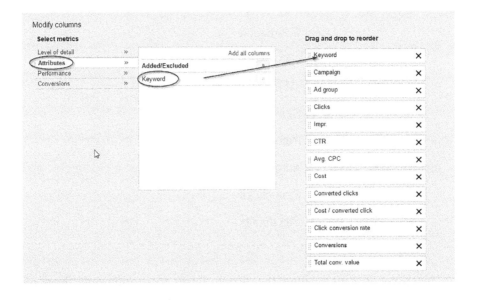

This will give you a view that looks like this:

Search Terms	Keyword ?	Campaign	Ad group	Clicks ?
manduca baby carrier	--	SEB - PLA - Main - Level 3	SEB2 -	8
mima winter kit	--	SEB - PLA - Main - Mima Xari Only	SEB3 -	4
baby brezza	--	SEB - PLA - Main - Level 3	Baby and Toddler	19
baby brezza formula pro uk	--	SEB - PLA - Main - Level 1 - Catch All	SEB3 -	1

You will notice that the Keyword column is filled with a blank (i.e., '--'). This is odd because when you export the list it looks like this:

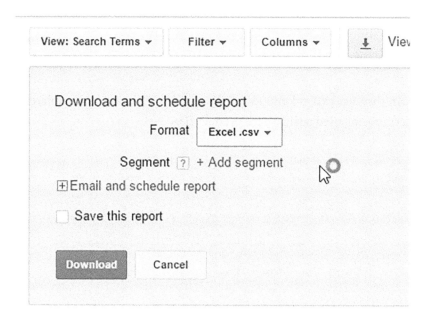

Search term report (1 Nov 2016-25 Nov 2016)			
Search term	Keyword		Campaign Ad group
soft light baby room	category_l1=537 and brand=meemoo and id=6673		SEB - PLA - SEB3 -
children's travelling potty	category_l1=537 and brand=my carry potty and id=6225		SEB - PLA - SEB3 -
nursing bras new look	category_l1=166 and brand=anna cecilia and id=5240		SEB - PLA - SEB3 -
mima xari buggies	id=5836		SEB - PLA - Top Mimi
mima xari buggies	category_l1=537 and brand=mima xari/kobi and id=6700		SEB - PLA - SEB3 -
fleece pram liner	category_l1=537 and brand=outlook and id=6353		SEB - PLA - SEB3 -
buggy board parts	category_l1=537 and brand=buggyboard, lascal and id=44		SEB - PLA - SEB3 -

As you can see, you get the Search Term against ID. But it's hard to work out the different IDs getting different search terms at this stage. So, add another column to the right of Keyword and then add in the formula:

Connections	Sort & Filter	Data Tools

=RIGHT(B3,LEN(B3)-FIND("id=",B3))

	B	C
Nov 2016)		
	Keyword	
	category_l1=537 and brand=meemoo and id=6673	=RIGHT(B3,LEN(B3)-FIND("id=",B3))
	category_l1=537 and brand=my carry potty and id=6225	
	category_l1=166 and brand=anna cecilia and id=5240	

This will make it look like this:

Keyword	
category_l1=537 and brand=meemoo and id=6673	d=6673
category_l1=537 and brand=my carry potty and id=6225	
category_l1=166 and brand=anna cecilia and id=5240	

You can then use this column to sort by product IDs and see the different search terms being used against each product ID.

mima xari pram	category_l1=537 and brand=mima and id=5949	d=5949	SEB - PLA	SEB3 -	15
mima prams for sale	category_l1=537 and brand=mima and id=5949	d=5949	SEB - PLA	SEB3 -	1
mima xari 3 in 1 pushchair	category_l1=537 and brand=mima and id=5949	d=5949	SEB - PLA	SEB3 -	1
mema pram	category_l1=537 and brand=mima and id=5949	d=5949	SEB - PLA	SEB3 -	1
mima pram	category_l1=537 and brand=mima and id=5949	d=5949	SEB - PLA	SEB3 -	22
mina pram	category_l1=537 and brand=mima and id=5949	d=5949	SEB - PLA	SEB3 -	2
xari	category_l1=537 and brand=mima and id=5949	d=5949	SEB - PLA	SEB3 -	1
mima xari uk 3 in 1	category_l1=537 and brand=mima and id=5949	d=5949	SEB - PLA	SEB3 -	1
mima xari stroller	category_l1=537 and brand=mima and id=5949	d=5949	SEB - PLA	SEB3 -	1
mima xari with car seat	category_l1=537 and brand=mima and id=5949	d=5949	SEB - PLA	SEB3 -	1
mima xari set	category_l1=537 and brand=mima and id=5949	d=5949	SEB - PLA	SEB3 -	1
mima uk	category_l1=537 and brand=mima and id=5949	d=5949	SEB - PLA	SEB3 -	1
momi xari	category_l1=537 and brand=mima and id=5949	d=5949	SEB - PLA	SEB3 -	1

With this information, you can make better decisions on whether the product title can be exchanged for the search terms to see if you can get more traffic.

Product Descriptions

Feed optimisation is really all about the product title. The description does not matter as much (in my experience); however, here are some things you can do to optimize the product description. You'll especially want to do this if you are in a highly competitive area and everything else is already optimized. Again, there's a conflict between what Google wants and what the website needs, so a specific description attribute for the Google description is a good idea. The most important part of the description is what appears first, so you can try adding keyword rich text here. However, this description should still make grammatical sense, and you should not try 'keyword stuffing,' which would make your product look spammy and not provide an ideal user experience.

Henry Natural Teak Dining Table
from Puji.com

Wood · Reclaimed Wood · Rectangular / Square

Dine in style with our best selling dining table. Hand crafted from solid Indonesian Reclaimed Teak and finish highlights the wonderful and rustic ...

See more details at Puji.com »

£775.00
+£40.00 shipping
Puji.com
★★★★⯨ (69)

Shop

Here the search keyword is 'teak dining table' and we can see this in the product title. It also appears naturally in the product description.

Consider also what search terms a Googler uses. For example, this product:

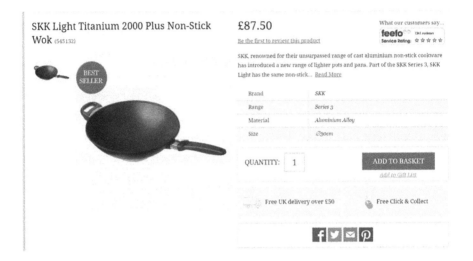

The product description describes the material – good – non-stick, etc. – but it doesn't mention size. The sizing information also might be listed as 12 cm or 30 cm, for example – but people don't often search this way.

Keyword (by relevance)		Avg. monthly searches [?]
large wok		170
small wok		110
14" wok		10
12" wok		10
30cm wok		40
medium wok		10

You can see that most people search for the term 'large wok' rather than 12-in or 30-cm wok, so your description should include this search term. You always want to help Google match the product to the searcher. If the size search term receives a large amount of traffic, consider adding it into the product title.

If you have lots of products, you can create rules to help you out programmatically. Take this product for example:

SKK Light Titanium 2000 Plus Non-Stick Saucepan - ⌀16cm (545019)

£60.00

Be the first to review this pro

Part of the SKK Series 3, these
an advanced Titanium 2000 F
casting process is the key to n

Brand

Range

Material

Size

Capacity

QUANTITY: 1

This is a 'medium saucepan,' so you could create an if/then rule that says:

"IF the product title has 'saucepan' and '16cm' contained in it"

THEN

"Append the word 'medium' in front of saucepan"

Using rules like this, you can add important information to your product titles in the Google product feed.

Colours – sometimes your shop will use fancy names for colours on the site like *teal* or *maroon* – translate these colours into their more commonly searched for term like *light blue* and *dark red* as this will get you more impressions.

Optimisation of Products for Different Search Queries

We've discovered that sometimes a product is suitable for targeting two or three high traffic keywords – targeting only one keyword would mean missing out on the other keywords and vice versa. In this case, we utilize different sizes or colours of the product on the site and optimize the different product variants for slightly different keywords. This technique tends to work well when a site has a lot of potential search terms but a small inventory of products.

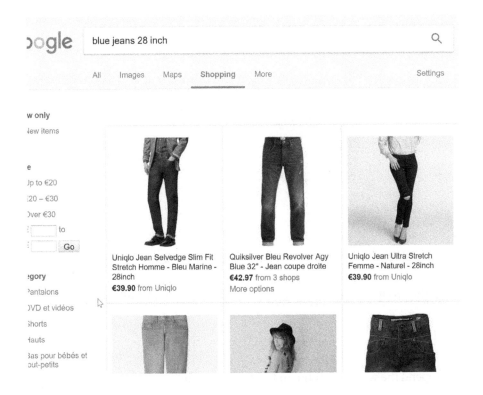

Categorisation

Google also depends on the product feed's ability to classify the products into the categories that will help them serve up the right products to the right audience. What Google needs for categorisation may be different from what the website needs for categories. For example, Google might have much more granular categories then the website or vice versa. Out of the box, most products are mapped to a category on the website, and then this category is mapped to a Google category.

So, a good way to optimize the feed is to have a separate field on each product called 'Google category.' This provides a lot more options to the Adword manager to control what product goes into which Google category. Some of the Google categories get broken down more than others, so these can be exploited well if this technique is used.

A good example of this is the website Brook Taverner. Although they don't have a category for tuxedos, they actually do sell the product, so we put the product in the following Google category:

Apparel & Accessories > Clothing > Suits > Tuxedos

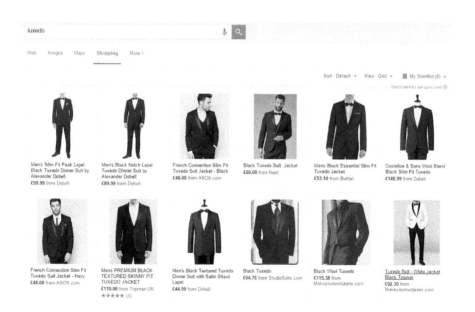

Search Intent

If you want to further optimize your feed, look for products that seem to sell whenever they are shown and the bottleneck is just how many impressions you can get. If you hone in on these products, you can ramp up your sales as many retailers make 80% of their revenue from 20% of their products – and sometimes it's even more extreme than this.

So, if you find these key products and work harder on these, you will get the results. Once you've found a target product, take time to research the search terms used for this product.

Let's say kettles are a big seller for your site, and for example, your kettles category looks like this:

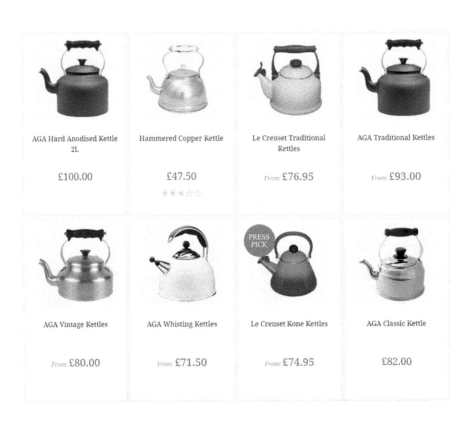

AGA Hard Anodised Kettle 2L	Hammered Copper Kettle	Le Creuset Traditional Kettles	AGA Traditional Kettles
£100.00	£47.50	*From:* £76.95	*From:* £93.00
	★ ★ ★ ☆ ☆		

| AGA Vintage Kettles | AGA Whisting Kettles | Le Creuset Kone Kettles | AGA Classic Kettle |
| *From:* £80.00 | *From:* £71.50 | *From:* £74.95 | £82.00 |

The product titles are using words such as 'traditional kettles' or 'vintage kettles' and 'whistling kettle.'

whistling kettle	1,600 High	£0.38	
stove top kettle	1,600 High	£0.46	
stove kettle	720 High	£0.38	
vintage kettle	390 High	£0.34	
traditional kettle	390 High	£0.49	»

As you can see, 'stove top' and 'whistling kettle' are the top terms. You want to have products that target each of these terms: i.e., it could actually be the same kettle but in a different colour and a slightly different product title.

Product Images

What images stand out and how can you test?

Unfortunately, the only way to split test different images is to alternate, using one image one day and another the next. Given the image is only updated each day in Google Merchant centre, this is as close to split testing as you can get. But day split testing can provide good enough results over a 10-day period for you to understand which image works best. You also need to do something to make it easier to track results, so you'll need to change the final URL to have a # on the end of it to designate which image is being used.

Example: www.amazingstore.com/product123.html#image1
And then the next day: www.amazingstore.com/product123.html#image2

By doing this, you can look in the dimensions reports and find out how these fair over a longer period of testing. You also have to remember to flip the images over each day.

Overall, though, common sense means that to get the click you must work to stand out more than the others. There are a variety of ways to do this, and here are some images that do just that:

This is an image of a Harris Tweed Jacket and it uses a small Harris Tweed logo in the top right corner to gain a little more attention. Usually, the logo must be over the product image for Google to accept it!

Also, for clothing, you'll want to try lifestyle images (aspirational images of model in stunning locations), model images (clothing on a person) or garment images (clothing folded on a shelf) to determine which ones work better for each type of clothing.

Mens Classic Long Sleeve
Formal Shirts Size S To 3xl -
Work Casual
£8.95 from eBay - azbags

This product image stands out as it shows all the colours available in the particular product.

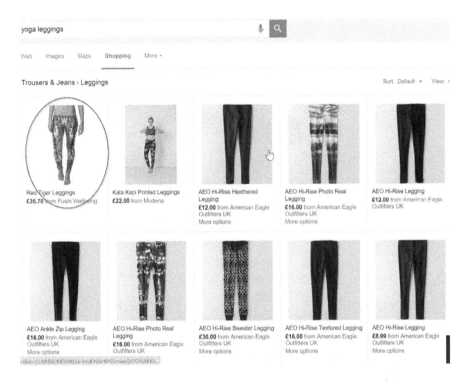

This product stands out because the image looks more professional, so it justifies the higher price tag. It's the clear choice for a more affluent buyer.

Just like testing for product titles is difficult using the AdWords interface, the same is true for image testing: i.e., finding out which image is better means downloading everything into Excel and working out the before and after. With a little tweaking, I am going to incorporate this into my 'before and after' title testing tool, and if people want to help with beta testing on this, please let me know!

Tools like Datafeedwatch do allow you to use the different alternative images as the main feed.

There is a feature that allows you to select which image is the one used as the image_link in the feed. Thus, you can use this to see which images get the best results in terms of click through rate and ultimately ROAS.

Pricing

Out of everything, if you are selling products that other people are selling, then price has a huge effect on your sales. So much so that a lower price and a lower bid is often better than a higher price and a higher bid. The bid you pay for the same traffic is much lower for a lower price.

Google uses the GTIN number to compare product prices and uses this to work out what to show for which query. The only time competitors will appear above you in the shopping results is if they have better seller reviews and their price is not too far from yours. The quality score for shopping seems to be heavily weighted for price.

Price is only important for products or brands that are sold by more than one online retailer. If you are selling your own brand, then there are other strategies that can generate more revenue overall. A higher price sometimes signals value to the user, and then discounting down against this high price with an offer can create motivation to buy today. We have used this technique for own brand products very effectively for a number of retailers.

Use of Offers and Promotions

Which offers get shown and which don't?

Shop for bathing suits on Google   Sponsored ⓘ

Victoria's Secret Zip Long Line...	Venus One-Piece Wo...	Soma Captiva Precious Dot...	coral mint two piece two tone...
$29.99	**$22.00**	**$19.99**	**$32.99**
Victoria's Secret	Venus	Soma Intimates	LolliCouture
🏷 Special offer	🏷 Special offer		

Offers are now being shown under the product – but it doesn't indicate what the offer is.

When you actually click on the offer, the deal will be revealed.

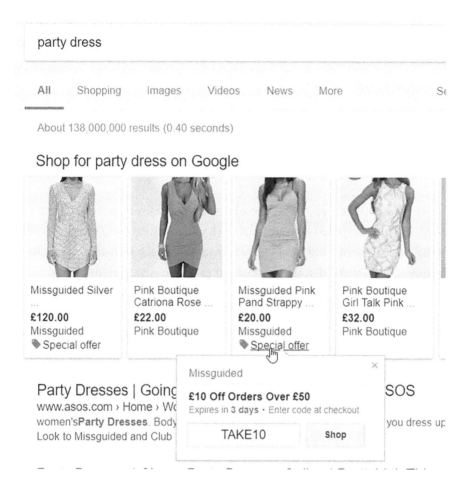

The good thing about this is that it prompts an increase in click through rates from the enticement of the offer, even though many people won't actually redeem the offer.

Offers do affect your ability to stand out from the crowd and will increase your click through rate (CTR). Offers should help reduce the cost per click you pay as your quality score increases. The types of offers we have tried and had success with are:

- Free delivery.
- Free delivery over a certain order value.
- BOGOF: buy one get one free.
- Tiered % discounts: i.e., spend £100 to get 10% off, spend £150 to get 15% off.

We have experienced the best results with free delivery; however, with the right account, the tiered discount can work well and increase the average order value. When I set up and ran Google Ads for one of the UK's largest jewellery businesses, the tiered discount turned out to be a license to print money.

The merchant centre reviews each promotion coupon manually, and this is a pain if you have a tight offer window: for example, Black Friday.

To get around this, the merchant centre created a new area called Promotion Feeds which allows you to create a feed detailing all the promotions you have coming up. This includes a field to allow you to show the promotion between select dates while the active date remains outside of these parameters.

For example, you can set the active date a few days before the coupon needs to go live so that Google can review the promotion before it needs to be shown. Why they don't add this to the normal promotions interface, I am not sure, but perhaps they want people to use feeds. However, I expect most people do what I do and submit a feed file based on a manual GoogleDoc spreadsheet. But the use of feeds can lead to a total automation of this process, tying in with, for example, Magento's promotions engine to create the promotions in the product feed and promotions feed without having to set anything up externally in the Merchant Centre. A word of advice: if promotions are going to be a huge part of the business and are going to be done on subsets of products all the time, automating this is going to remove a lot of headaches.

When to Use Offers & with Which Types of Clients

If you sell commoditized products (products that many other retailers sell) and they are exactly the same product, then using onsite discounts with coupons is not going to work because people will only click on the products that have the lowest price or come within a range. If your discount uses a coupon, then the price seen in Google Shopping will be a higher price than the competition, so Google will not show your product as much. For example: if you sell Samsung 2345 TVs, then make sure your price is the lowest and only use the promotions for 'free shipping' type offers.

However, if you sell a product that you are the manufacturer of and nobody really knows you, then you can use a higher price to set a reference point for high value and then use a coupon to discount down against this. We have found this method to work well with brands that customers haven't heard of – setting a higher price as a signal for value and then discounting down against this to create a sense of urgency for the buyer.

This is a good example of Pavlovian association bias if you want to read more around the psychology of buying behaviour.

You can only have promotions that use a coupon code or do something specific to the price on the basket page that normal shoppers don't receive. For example, if you have a before and after price on the product page, then this type of promotion cannot be used. To use a promotion, the price in the feed and the price on the product pages need to be the same and the offer needs to be applied at the checkout, either via a coupon or automatically.

You can either apply the promotion to all products or a subset of products. Often, my clients want to use a coupon code to discount a category of products or individual products. To do this you can use the promo field in the Google Shopping Feed and enter values for a particular promotion in there. For example, if you wanted to have a 50% off coupon that applied only to wooden sheds, then you might put the promo name 'woodsheds50' in the promotion field. Then, in the merchant centre in the promotions area, you can reference this promo name and set up the promotion for only those products.

The delay in approval can be significant if the promotion is only valid for one day. Take Black Friday for example, which is only one day. If you don't give

Google enough time to approve the coupon, you could miss the promotion window. So, it's best to set up the coupon to work prior to the official go live day and give Google plenty of time to approve it. Google is getting faster and often reviews the code that same day, but for big days, like Black Friday, I imagine they get swamped!

What's difficult is figuring out the impact of a promotion on certain products. For example, does the CTR improve, do sales improve, and if so, which promotion works best? To see this information you'll have to make a note of the promotion's go live date and then pull the reports against product IDs in the dimensions area.

Custom Labels to Give You an Edge

You are able to have five different custom label fields. These are 0, 1, 2, 3, and 4, and you can put any value into these fields that you want. I often use these fields to add in identifiers for each product so that I can split up the campaign product groups the way I want. However, you can also use these fields to add important information that can affect your bidding.

A good example would be an item that has just gone on sale or is suddenly selling well. If this is a product that normally doesn't sell, you may have already bid down the product so that it's not receiving many impressions – so, left to run its own course, it will take a long time for Google to recognize that this product is now selling well and also for you to realize that this product should be bid up. If you have a custom field that includes the date that an item went on sale you could write an AdWords script to watch for this and to automatically bid up that product, maybe by 100%. You can then specify another field to show when an item comes off sale to bid the product back down. This way you can automate the coming and going of sales, especially if a retailer has different categories and SKUs going into promotion at different times.

A good idea, which I heard on a recent webinar, is to use a 5% off offer just to get the higher click through rate on the advertisement. You can often get this click through benefit without the coupon being used. This is because Google's method of showing the coupon code to a shopper is quite cumbersome, and therefore, many just see the special offer, become interested and click through to buy, completely forgetting about the offer. Worth testing though!

Labels Based on 'Bestseller' Status

Having a label to highlight 'bestseller' status is a great way to use custom labels. For example, a product might be very seasonal and might start selling well on the store generally. Google won't automatically know that this product will sell well, so you'll want to pre-empt this and push this product harder given that it should be selling well due to the season of fashion, etc. You could have a 'bestsellers' score from 1–10 in the field that you use to either manually bid higher or script it to do a kind of bid modifier.

Item ID	Campaign	Custom label 4	Ad group	Clic
5829	SEB - Shopping - Rangemaster inventory	bestseller	Rangemaster - Rangemaster	
4681	SEB - Shopping Main - Catch All - D	lowseller	SEB2 -	
1184	SEB - Shopping Main - Catch All - D	bestseller	SEB2 -	
3422	SEB - Shopping Main - Catch All - D	lowseller	SEB2 -	
7054	SEB - Shopping Main - Catch All - D	lowseller	SEB2 -	
765	SEB - Shopping Main - Catch All - D	lowseller	SEB2 -	
5739	SEB - Shopping - Rangemaster inventory	lowseller	Rangemaster - Rangemaster	

Labels Based on Price Checking

If you sell a lot of products that other people sell, then using a price matching tool such as www.prisync.com allows you to monitor the pricing on other websites. This becomes interesting when you use the API of Prisync to dynamically add into your product feed the price competitiveness of the product.

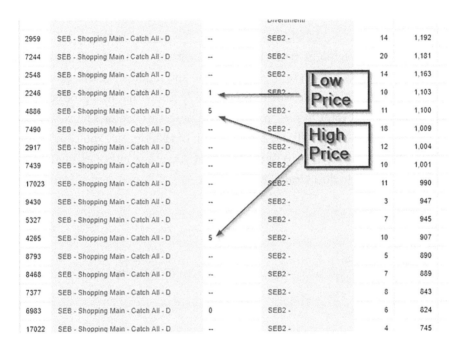

For example, we added to the product feed the following values as a custom label for each product:

- **All Equal Price** – The product was the same price as the others price matched.
- **Best or 2nd** – The product was competitively priced either the lowest price or second lowest.
- **Higher Priced** – The product was higher priced than the competition.
- **Not Price Matched** – No data.

We could then clearly see the effect on the click through rate, the conversion rate based on these values.

In some industries, pricing is very important and can change multiple times per day. If this is the case, you will need to use Google's Inventory Feed. This is a separate feed that just contains the product IDs, the stock level and the price. This gets refreshed much more often than the basic product feed and thus allows you to stay up to date with Google much more easily. Using this feed also opens the ability to conduct hour-by-hour split testing on prices to see where you should be in terms of price: i.e., high price one hour then low price the next. This is not as effective as real-time split testing, but it's as close as we can get, and we have gleaned excellent insights from it, especially for merchants selling their own brand of products.

You want to be pushing products that are priced well and have a chance of selling. If the product is too expensive, it's not going to sell. By using an API to a price tracking tool and then using AdWords Scripting to base the bid on the price of the product, you can automate this process. This method can save a huge amount of overspend and give you a favourable edge in the market.

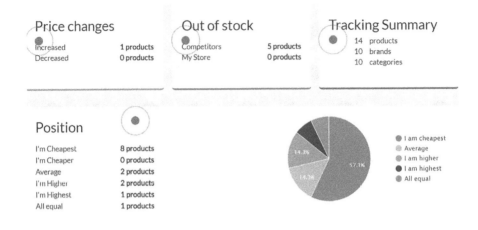

The biggest hurdle to this technique is getting the data on the competitors to price match.

Labels Based on Margin of the Product

Some merchants have hugely different profit margins on different products. Some products are even loss leaders and sold to entice buyers. Other products are only stocked to support others, such as spare parts, and sold as a contractual agreement to have rights to sell the 'big' products. In a nutshell, it can get messy.

With these types of merchants you have two options in terms of optimisation. These are as follows:

- Instead of passing the full revenue of the product when sold to Google AdWords as the sale amount, pass the margin made: i.e., Product Profit Margin = Product Sale Revenue – Product Cost. Then, in AdWords, you have the product profit margin and bidding changes. Optimisations can be based around this data. This is the best option; however, many merchants don't have this information in their stores. Usually, it's in the ERP system but not in their ecommerce store. Hence, it's a lot of work for them to get this into the feed, and often, it just doesn't happen.

- If the merchant can't put this into their product feed at product level, then you can use rules to assign a value as a custom label. For example, one of our merchants knows roughly how much margin they have on the various brands they sell:

Brand 1 – 20% margin

Brand 2 – 22% margin

Brand 3 – 30% margin

I would then turn these into labels, such as

Very High Margin

Medium Margin

Normal Margin

Lower Margin

No Margin

Item ID	Campaign	Custom label 3 [?]	Ad group	Clicks
3373	SEB - Shopping Main Level 3 - D	--	SEB2 -	
3420	SEB - Shopping Main Level 3 - D	--	SEB2 -	
1993	SEB - Shopping Main - Catch All - D	highmargin	SEB2 -	
2067	SEB - Shopping Main - Catch All - D	--	SEB2 -	
2227	SEB - Shopping Main - Catch All - D	--	SEB2 -	
2653	SEB - Shopping Main - Catch All - D	highmargin	SEB2 -	
2714	SEB - Shopping Main - Catch All - D	--	SEB2 -	
2824	SEB - Shopping Main - Catch All - D	--	SEB2 -	
2825	SEB - Shopping Main - Catch All - D	--	SEB2 -	
2827	SEB - Shopping Main - Catch All - D	--	SEB2 -	
2881	SEB - Shopping Main - Catch All - D	--	SEB2 -	
3195	SEB - Shopping Main - Catch All - D	--	SEB2 -	
3521	SEB - Shopping Main - Catch All - D	--	SEB2 -	

Using these margins per brands, you can create rules (using a tool like DataFeedWatch) to create IF statements to add in the correct margin for the product. You can then split your product groups via this custom field for bidding purposes.

Item ID	Campaign	Conv. value / cost ↓ [?]	Ad group
765	SEB - Shopping Main - Catch All - D	3,750.00	SEB2 -
1184	SEB - Shopping Main - Catch All - D	549.17	SEB2 -
7054	SEB - Shopping Main - Catch All - D	30.82	SEB2 -

Also, you can pull off reports using dimensions to work out the return on advertised spend (ROAS) on the different margin levels and make sure that you're getting top results for the client. For example, you would be able to tolerate a lower ROAS on a high-margin product.

Labels Based on Lifetime Customer Value

For some clients, lifetime customer value is very important. Take a merchant selling health supplements, for example. Certain supplements can easily turn into a repeat purchase every month; others might be a one time purchase. Google doesn't know which products lead to repeat sales, so it's hard to bid for maximum profit. If you only have a few products, you will likely know which products have a history of leading to repeat purchases, but if you have thousands of products, this becomes more complicated.

Another tool? Of course!

We developed a stats tool that measures the lifetime value against each product. So, if someone buys SKU 123, we can calculate on average how much this person spends in a year. We then use an XML feed to get this information into a custom label in the product feed. Once it's there, we can bid based on the lifetime value of a product rather than on the first sale.

This information can be very revealing, and you might be willing to incur a small loss on the first sale if you knew you were going to make a large amount out of that new customer in the long run.

How to Test These Different Custom Labels

Ideally, you want to find some correlation between the custom label values you add and conversion rate or return on spend: i.e., if one of your customer labels shows whether it's currently a bestseller for something trendy like fashion, then you might expect a higher conversion rate for trending items. If you find this correlation, you can use bid modifiers to change the product bid based on the current label and to change the bid if the label changes.

So, once you have custom label values in place, let them run for 30 days or more, and then pull off the sales information using the dimensions report in the following way:

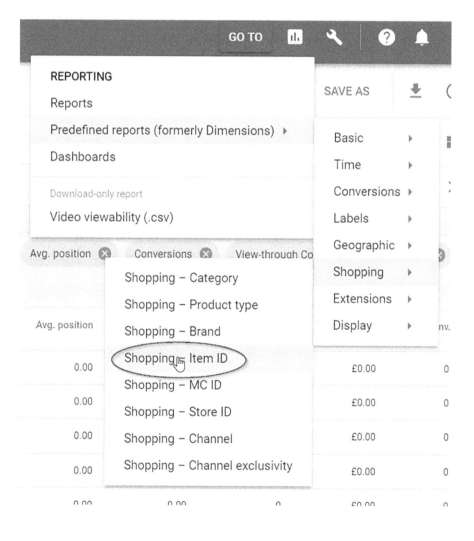

Then modify the columns that you can see:

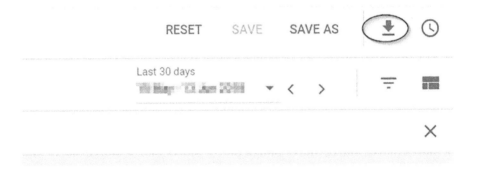

To include the custom labels, add in the custom labels you are using, then export to Excel:

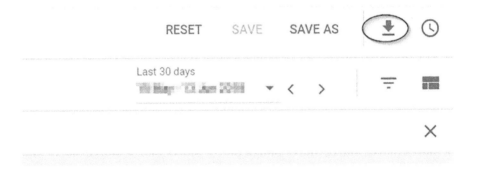

Open in Excel, and then select all the data apart from the top row that contains the date of the data. Also, don't include the totals in the bottom row.

	F	G	H	I	J	K
4432	0.97%	0.05	0.1	0	0	0.
4433	0.00%	0	0	0	0	0.
4434	1.54%	0.35	0.7	0	0	0.
4435	1.47%	0.54	22.31	3	7.44	7.
4436	0.00%	0	0	0	0	0.
4437	1.32%	0.23	6.43	0	0	0.
4438	1.25%	0.24	0.71	0	0	0.
4439	0.00%	0	0	0	0	0.
4440	0.68%	0.06	0.06	0	0	0.

Insert a pivot table, and then create a table like this:

Row Labels	Sum of Clicks	Sum of Cost	Sum of Impressions	Sum of Converted clicks	Sum of Total conv. value
--	1	0.33	129	0	0
bestseller	4830	1924.58	296406	185	7935.13
lowseller	14205	4345.02	1148629	385	19933
Grand Total	19036	6269.93	1445164	570	27868.13

Copy and paste this data onto a new sheet, and work out things like conversion rate, return on spend, etc.

Row Labels	ConvR	ROAS
--		
bestseller	3.83%	412.30%
lowseller	2.71%	458.76%
Grand Total	2.99%	444.47%

Once you can see the conversion rates and ROAS, you can make a decision on whether you want to script bid modifiers. In the above example, while the conversion rate is higher for the 'bestseller' label, the return on spend is lower.

Another attribute you might want to use in a custom label is 'stock levels,' to see if they affect conversion rates. For example, what happens when you only have three or four items left, compared to 20? If this is shown on your product page, when stock is low, it might cause a scarcity trigger that increases conversion rate. If you can find a correlation here, then you might want to bid higher when stock levels get low, or vice versa.

THIRD PARTY TOOLS

Once you have the basics right and you know what you are doing, you will want to learn some time-saving techniques. It's very well optimising a product set of 80 products, but when you have thousands, then you need to start automating.

However, I always say start manually and then become consistent. Only once you understand what you want done would I venture out into these third-party areas.

A good example of where tools and scripts can work well is with bidding strategy. Once you have a method of bidding, be it based on the overall product groups, customer label selection, etc., then you will want to have a crack at automating at least some of it.

I am going to cover Time and Day Bidding and look at uses of Google AdWords Scripting, but beware, nothing messes up an account faster than a script gone haywire.

OPTMYZR

If you start managing large campaigns, then you might want to use a tool like Optmyzr that has some bulk editing tools for Google Shopping. Its tools that I've found useful follow:

• Shopping Bidder

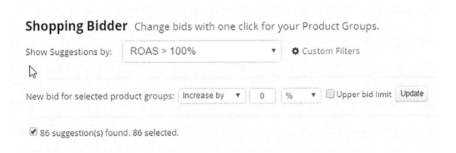

With this tool you can change the bids en masse, using criteria based on filters. For example, you can bid up products that have achieved a return on advertised spend of over four by 10%: i.e., push the products that are doing well harder. The reverse is true also. You can show products that are spending and not converting and bid these down. I tend to bid up and down products based on the clients ROAS targets and then seek out my 'superstar' products and bid these up manually to make sure I am getting the most from these products.

While I don't use this on most of my accounts, as I have built a bidding engine that works via Google AdWords Scripting, I do use this bidding method for new accounts. I like to start everything manually until I get a feel for the account.

- Shopping Campaign Builder

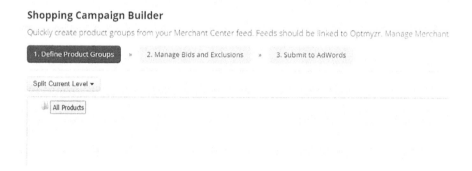

This is a great tool to use when you are creating your campaigns as you can quickly build out structures on the fly and then press a button to build these out in your AdWords account.

- Shopping Campaign Refresher

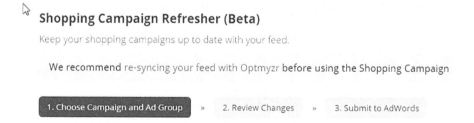

This tool allows you to sync your Google Shopping Campaign structure with the product feed. At first glance, this is not obvious because you would assume that Google would have maintained this itself, but it does not. Let's say you split products into product groups using the Brand field:

- Nike
- Reebok
- Adidas

Next, each brand product group is split by Product ID. When you create these product groups, all is fine, but what happens if another Nike product is added to the feed? Well, instead of it being put into the Nike product groups, it gets put in the 'everything else.' This is annoying because without constant management you can end up with a lot of brand-specific products in the 'everything else' group, especially when a season changes and new stock appears. So what Optmyzr does is look for products that should be in the set product groups and then adds them in for you. This saves a lot of time and bother. However, if you have a website that adds lots of new SKUs daily, then having to login to Optmyzr every day to do this can be tedious. So, for these types of clients, we have had to go down the scripted route: i.e., a script running every day to match the product groups with the feed. This has worked really well, making sure that the bidding for the types of products added is correct.

BIDDING STRATEGY

Bidding Using Enhanced Bidding

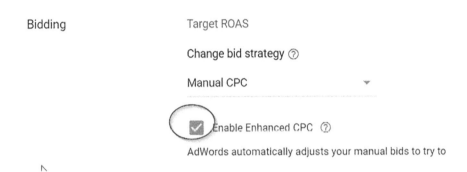

Bidding   Target ROAS

                               Change bid strategy ⑦

                               Manual CPC   ▼

                               ☑ Enable Enhanced CPC ⑦
                               AdWords automatically adjusts your manual bids to try to

In the settings for each shopping campaign, there is a selection to be made around bidding type. I have found that enhanced bidding can work quite well once Google has a decent chunk of history to use. Similar to CPA bidding on normal text adverts, you have to monitor it as it can go off the boil as the data changes.

> Here's what Google said about **Enhanced CPC** when it was launched:
>
> *"If you want to manage your own bids or use a third-party bidding platform, enhanced CPC is your best bet. It dynamically optimizes on top of your bid in real-time, so you get more conversions or sales at a similar cost.*
>   *"We're seeing advertisers get as many as 7% more conversions at the same cost with eCPC!" (Google 2015)*

Because this bidding method takes into account context and auction dynamics at the time of the click, Google can optimize the click to increase the performance of your shopping campaign: i.e., Google will boost your bid when it thinks it will most likely get a conversion and vice versa.

However, Google has now announced that the cap it uses for bids, which used to be no more than 30% of your bid, is now being removed. Therefore, they could effectively bid whatever they wanted. In removing this cap, it moves this default bidding method much closer to the other bidding models they provide.

The issue with this is that the S curve of improvement in sales diminishes after a while in raising a bid, and Google will have a bias to spend more.

If you want to go further into bid management in Google Shopping, you have the following options available:

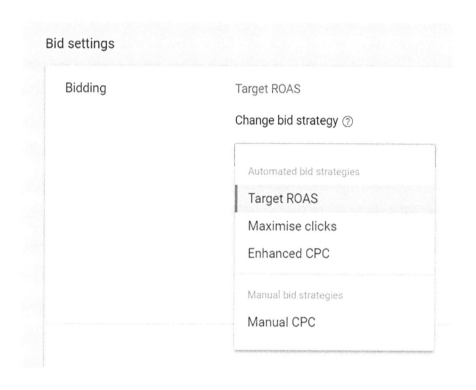

This appears under Flexible Bidding strategy. Personally, I am still experimenting with this and have found that a lot of the time ROAS can do very well, but sometimes it can totally fail too. But, as mentioned before, if you get a bestseller campaign working on some optimized products, then these bid models can work well.

Time and Day Bidding

Google Shopping allows you to bid differently at different times of the day. In order to gain insight into when to bid higher and lower, you want to pull off about three months worth of data, looking at 'conversion value / cost' against time of day and day of the week. This way, you'll be able to see when you get the most return on your ad spend and when you don't. I tend to find that some times during the week people are more likely to buy certain products and also that certain shopping times bring different shopper types. Different shopping types have different buying habits, and if you have limited budget, you want to be hitting the buyer types who have the highest average order value.

Hint: Bid more when the whales are out shopping and hold back on the minnows.

Annoyingly, Google AdWords only lets you see data according to either time of day aggregate or day of week aggregate and not both at the same time.

I'm sure you can get this data using Google Analytics and setting up custom reports, but when I tried it, the cost information did not come through, so I am going to show you this technique using the Optmyzr tool:

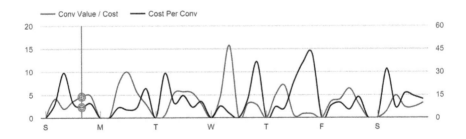

Plotted above in blue (the lighter line), we can see the times of day and days of the week when we generate the most revenue for our spend.

Conversion Value / Cost shows that:

- Midday Monday is a good time to bid more.
- Monday overall is quite good.
- Wednesday morning is great.
- Thursday morning is pretty good.

So, based on this, we might want to mirror our bidding strategy as follows:

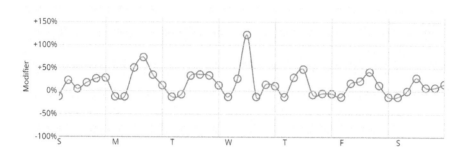

Here we are maximising the bidding when optimal and reducing when poor. If you don't have revenue information in your Google Shopping account (i.e., if you are crazy) or if every conversion is the same, then you can optimize in the same way by bidding against the opposite of cost per conversion.

I tend to rejig this bidding at the end of each month to adjust for different buying habits at different times of the year. For example, people spend differently at different times during Christmas than they do during the normal run of the year, so you would want to be more tuned in to this bidding graph at this time, making more adjustments more often.

Google AdWords Scripting

Google AdWords scripting allows you to really expand your efforts when managing your campaign. A lot of the management can be scripted, leaving you to focus on the more strategic things in the account. Scripting is so powerful that it can often do a better, more refined job than doing it manually can. But I say that with a caveat as you have to really understand what you want your scripts to do before you get them implemented. I use a technique manually for about two months across many accounts and do exactly what I want the script to do each week. Doing this, I get to find all the little things that can go wrong. Once I'm certain that everything is stable and working well, then I write a script. The things I have used scripts for are as follows:

- To automate the tiered keywords in the high-, medium- or low-bid campaigns. The script moves up and down the keywords based on their recent performance.
- Bidding on the product IDs based on recent performance.
- Location bidding.
- Hunting for keyword and product ID matches and creating the equivalent search ad and product landing page.
- Anomaly checking in an account to watch for major changes in sales or conversion rates.
- Day of the week and hour of the day bid modifiers.
- Moving products in and out of bestseller campaigns.

Bidding for Mobile & Tablets

Google recently rolled out device bidding for tablets, desktops and mobile. Before, you could only bid differently on mobile while desktop and tablets were lumped together. Now, you can have separate campaigns for each device. This could prove to be very beneficial, but only if you have at least 50 conversions per device per month. For example, you might find that certain high-priced items are rarely purchased on a mobile device, so having a separate campaign for mobile means that you can bid down these products.

I used to tend to split my shopping campaign by device and have tiers and bestseller campaigns for each device. But recently, with the Google Machine Learning getting better and better, it's often better to bunch things up and let the AI model do the work for you.

☐   ●   ▶ BT Shopping Level 2 - Jackets [D]

☐   ●   ▶ BT Shopping Level 2 - Jackets [M]

☐   ●   ▶ BT Shopping Level 2 - Jackets [T]

RLSA for Shopping Search

Remarketing lists of search adverts can be used very well in conjunction with shopping search. What this feature allows you to do is layer over bid modifiers on your normal shopping campaigns and bid differently based on past visitor behaviour. You can bid based on remarketing lists created in Google Analytics or bid based on a customer list of emails uploaded into Google AdWords.

Think of the following scenarios:

A customer who bought over a year ago is searching for a new hat.
- Given that this customer knows our store and has bought from us before, they are more likely to buy – thus, we might be able to put products in front of them for search terms that we have made negative for normal searchers. Therefore, we might have a separate shopping campaign set to 'target and bid' for existing customers. For example, because this is a customer who knows and likes us, then we can bid on more generic terms. If you have a huge customer list, you can segment the customer list even further into tiers based on frequency and recency. People who bought more recently and more frequently are worth bidding more on.

Someone who visited the website and spent over 6 minutes 10 days ago on the website is now searching again for those products on Google.

- It's likely that their first visit was part of their purchase research phase for making a purchase. They spent a lot of time on the website and thus were very engaged with the products that we sell. It's important, now that they are closer to making a buying decision, that we get our products back in front of them, so we can make the sale.

A customer who has recently added a product to the cart but not bought is now searching on Google Shopping for those products.

- This customer liked a product so much that they added something to the basket. What happened? They may have forgotten, but given that they are an engaged user of the website, it makes sense to bid higher for this traffic.

A customer who has already bought your main product is searching on Google.

- Let's say you sell a main high-priced product and once someone has bought that product the sales value is much lower. Perhaps you sell spa pools, and customers after this product don't buy much online. Therefore, you might bid down customers who have already bought the main product to not overspend on them while targeting new customers instead.

I tend to use the following remarketing lists to allow me bid up for certain visitors:

- Visitors who have spent more than 6 minutes on the site within the last 3 days
- Visitors who have spent more than 6 minutes on the site within the last 7 days
- Visitors who have spent more than 6 minutes on the site within the last 15 days
- Visitors who have spent more than 6 minutes on the site within the last 30 days
- Visitors who have spent more than 6 minutes on the site within the last 90 days
- Visitors who have spent more than 2 minutes on the site within the last 3 days
- Visitors who have spent more than 2 minutes on the site within the last 7 days
- Visitors who have spent more than 2 minutes on the site within the last 15 days
- Visitors who have spent more than 2 minutes on the site within the last 30 days
- Visitors who have spent more than 2 minutes on the site within the last 90 days
- Visitors who have spent less than 2 minutes on the site within the last 3 days
- Visitors who have spent less than 2 minutes on the site within the last 7 days
- Visitors who have spent less than 2 minutes on the site within the last 15 days
- Visitors who have spent less than 2 minutes on the site within the last 30 days
- Visitors who have spent less than 2 minutes on the site within the last 90 days
- Buyers within the last 540 days
- Customer email list

Start using 0% bid modifiers, just to see how each segment performs, and then after 30 days, you can see how much more the return on spend is for these segments and bid them up or down. Some of my RLSA bid modifiers are plus 300%, but I tend to move up or down in 25% increments.

MAJOR FEED CHANGES

Whenever you make large changes to the feed, it can take Google time to accept the feed and understand how best to optimize it. This can be challenging because when you make changes to a feed and the structure of the account, even if the structure is better, you may experience an immediate dip. We have seen this happen a lot when Google introduces a new requirement in the feed – such as the requirement for clothing to have one product for each size: i.e., the clothing feeds we have went from having 2,000 products to 8,000 products overnight. When questioned about how long Google would take to get used to the new feed, this is how they responded:

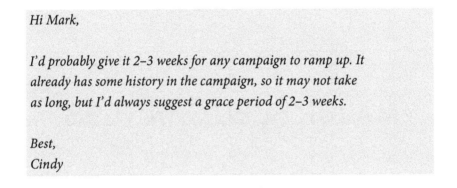

Hi Mark,

I'd probably give it 2–3 weeks for any campaign to ramp up. It already has some history in the campaign, so it may not take as long, but I'd always suggest a grace period of 2–3 weeks.

Best,
Cindy

Google

Hi Mark,

I'd probably give it 2-3 weeks for any campaign to ramp up. It already has some history in the campaign, so it may not take as long but I'd always suggest a grace period of 2-3 weeks.

Best,
Cindy

| Google Ireland Ltd. | The Google AdWords Team | 0-800-169-0409 | adwords.google.com |

We're here to help   Call   Email   Chat   Ask Experts   Help Center

So, if you do make big changes that you know are better, don't freak out if you have a dip for the first three weeks. You may have to go through a period of poor performance before you see results. When I first started working on shopping campaigns, I often rolled back my changes thinking that I had killed the account!

Decision Tree

A good way to work out how you want to manage a Google Shopping account is to map out a decision tree showing the changes you will make to what, and when you'll make them.

I have included two sample decision trees, so you can see the thinking process. I tend to map these out for new clients when I take them on so that I can see potentials for automation via scripting, as well as where I need to focus my attention. Once refined, you can also work out how often you are going to check each branch, e.g. once a day, once a week or once a month.

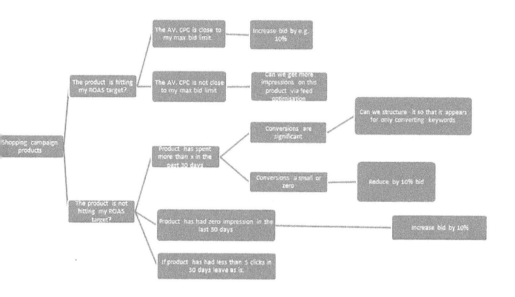

TAKING GOOGLE SHOPPING
TO THE NEXT LEVEL

When I saw the presentation on tiered Google Shopping campaigns, I thought 'that's it, that's the secret,' so I rolled this technique out across my campaigns. Year on year my results were better and I experienced incremental gains but not the huge leaps as shown in the presenter's chart. I wanted BIG gains, so I went hunting. Eventually, I came across something big by mistake.

First, it's always good to channel Charlie Munger and look at the inverse: i.e., 'what makes my campaigns worse' and given my random experiments I had plenty of these!

If we take a step back, all we can hope for with everything kept equal is to get a higher impression share for our best performing products. So, for example, we might have 20% of the products that drive most of the revenue and then a subset of these that do really well in terms of return on spend. You often have some products that the customer would want to sell 'all day every day' because they make so much money on them. These 'super' products in an un-optimized account usually have 20%–50% impression share. So, in order to 'crack' an account, we need a way to get more impressions for these products.

In order to understand how to do this, I would like to take you through the process which led me to work this secret out.

If you remember, earlier in the book I said that I tried putting each product ID into its own ad group and that this massively reduced my conversions.

Looking at this account, what was odd was that the impression share stayed the same, but I received more impressions:

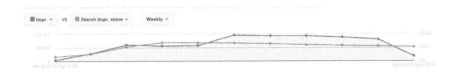

The first part of the year was seasonal, but the rest of the year wasn't. It's clear that just looking at the impression share doesn't really tell you how much traffic Google has.

But, when I rolled out one ad group per product ID, the following happened:

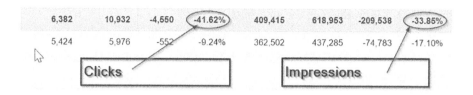

| 6,382 | 10,932 | -4,550 | -41.62% | 409,415 | 618,953 | -209,538 | -33.85% |
| 5,424 | 5,976 | -552 | -9.24% | 362,502 | 437,285 | -74,783 | -17.10% |

Clicks   Impressions

My clicks went down by 42% and my impressions down by 34%. WOW. I also had clients calling me at all hours to ask where their sales were!

This was the first clue.

Next, in another account, I brought out a group of products based on a category and then:

	Total conv. value ?		
01/09/2016 - 30/11/2016	03/06/2016 - 31/08/2016	Change	Change (%)
27,393.67	13,827.86	13,565.81	98.10%

Boom!!! Yes, I got a 100% increase in revenue from Shopping Search.

I did end up spending more but on roughly the same return on spend. The client was happy because they wanted more sales at the same ROAS. But previously Google was not giving me any more impressions.

Suddenly, I was getting more impressions from Google for the products that sold well.

Why was this?

Like all epiphanies, the answer came to me when I was relaxed. I was enjoying a massage by one of those Chinese dudes that stick his elbow in your neck, and suddenly the answer came to me.

It's all about click through rate on the ad group!

Google seems to take the click through rate of the ad group in aggregate and apply this to all the products and product groups in that ad group to determine the impressions that it gives the whole ad group. Therefore, you might have some really high CTR products that have a high ROAS which are being thwarted by the lower CTR products in the ad group.

This led me to a rule of thumb when deciding whether to take out a product group and put it into its own ad group. If the product group has a good ROAS and has a higher CTR then the current ad group that it's currently in, then it will more than likely do better on its own.

This also makes it vitally important to find products that get high impressions but low CTR and exclude them from the ad group so that the CTR of the ad group is not adversely affected.

So, if you want a product to sell more but it's got a low CTR, put it in an ad group with some products that have a high CTR so that they give the overall ad group a better score. However, usually you find that high ROAS products have a decent enough CTR.

Just knowing this information makes it so much easier to be strategic with your shopping campaigns. You understand the importance of CTR and which products sell well. You want to end up with an ad group that is your super selling ad group where you put your best products.

Like any business, go for what is working and try to get more sales from your best performing products first. So, look to see if you can improve the picture of the high ROAS products to get a high CTR. Hone in on the competition to see why people might click on their products – look at pricing, filters used on the image, size of image and product title. Really spend your time on the top products and optimize these. It will pay off as this is where you can get huge gains.

Using this technique and focusing on how the CTR will change based on the structure has allowed me to double Shopping revenue, sometimes in under a month if the client has the budget.

You can get even more advanced by looking at the 'benchmark' CTR to see if you get a better click through rate than the competition because if your CTR is higher than the benchmark and higher than the existing ad group then bringing it out into its own ad group should give it rocket boosters!

It also makes you sell products that get high impressions but low CTR by forcing you to consider what you can change – image, product title, promotion and product review stars to get this CTR up so it's not pulling the account down. Also, you'll be considering which keywords have high impressions but low

CTR and asking yourself if you should move them to the 'short tail' campaign, negative them out or optimize the product title to be a better match.

SUMMARY

All in all, this book is a blueprint filled with discoveries that took me years (and plenty of brain picking) to gain. If you treat it like the gem of information that it is, you can use it to greatly improve your Google Shopping revenue. You can double it, triple it or even better than that!

I want you to succeed, and I'd love your feedback. If you have found this black box of Google Shopping to be useful or if you have questions, please drop me a line at: mark.hammersley@smartebusiness.co.uk

Thank you for reading and good luck!

Mark Hammersley is a director of Global
Ecommerce agency Smartebusiness. He has worked
in Ecommerce for over 15 years for clients including
Naked Wines, AGA, Siemens and Comic Relief.

Lightning Source UK Ltd.
Milton Keynes UK
UKHW02f2024081018
330212UK00013B/1097/P